Withdrawn/ABCL MAR 2 0 2007

D0744206

Withdrawn/ABCL MAR 2 0 2007

Withdrawn/ABCL

3 9075 03615078 4

CARING FOR THE PLANET
TROPICAL RAIN FORESTS

Neil Champion

A⁺
Smart Apple Media

Published by Smart Apple Media
2140 Howard Drive West, North Mankato, MN 56003

Design and production by Helen James

Photographs by Getty Images (Jose Azel / Aurora, Dr R Howard Berg, James
P. Blair / National Geographic, Tim Chapman, China Photos, Nicole Duplaix /
National Geographic, Victor Englebert / Time Life Pictures, Peter Essick / Aurora,
Tim Graham, Sarah Leen / National Geographic, Romilly Lockyer, MAYELA
LOPEZ / AFP, H. John Maier Jr. / Image Works / Time Life Pictures, Michael
Melford / National Geographic, Michael Nichols / National Geographic, Michael
K. Nichols / National Geographic, JOEL NITO / AFP, ISSOUF SANOGO / AFP, Joel
Sartore / National Geographic, Maria Stenzel / National Geographic, Roy Toft /
National Geographic, Carl D. Walsh / Aurora, Steve Winter / National Geographic,
Paul A. Zahl / National Geographic)

Copyright © 2007 Smart Apple Media.
International copyright reserved in all countries. No part of this book may be
reproduced in any form without written permission from the publisher.

Library of Congress Cataloging-in-Publication Data

Champion, Neil.
Tropical rain forests / by Neil Champion.
p. cm. — (Caring for the planet)
ISBN-13 : 978-1-58340-508-6
1. Rain forests—Juvenile literature. 2. Rain forest ecology—Juvenile
literature. I. Title. II. Series.
QH86.C49 2006
577.34—dc22   2004056620

First Edition

9 8 7 6 5 4 3 2 1

Contents

Earth is an amazing place. It is complex, beautiful, and awe-inspiring. There has been life on it for some three and a half billion years. In all that time, it has grown more complex as life-forms **evolved**. Today, there are more species of plants and animals—about 10 million according to one scientific estimate—and more **habitats** in which they live than at any point in Earth's long history. This is our inheritance. It is this that we are changing at a faster rate than ever before. Our ability to alter the environment to suit our own purposes has never been greater. This allows many of us to live longer, more active lives. These are positive things. However, there are sides to our development and expansion that are not so positive for the planet.

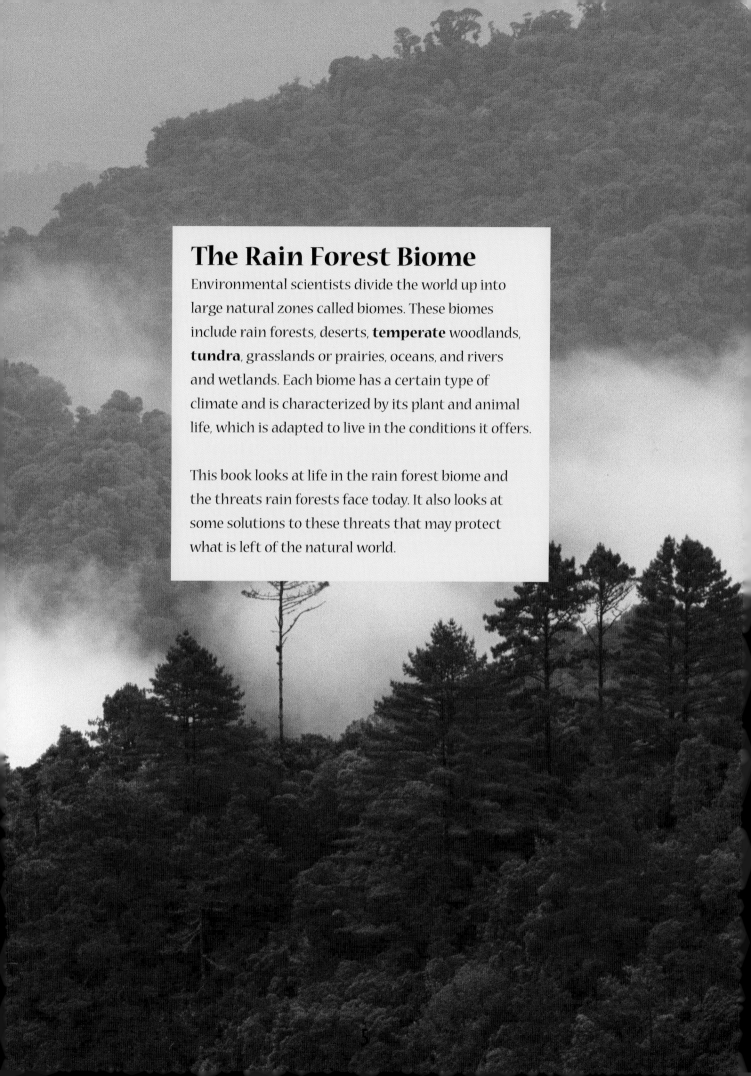

The Rain Forest Biome

Environmental scientists divide the world up into large natural zones called biomes. These biomes include rain forests, deserts, **temperate** woodlands, **tundra**, grasslands or prairies, oceans, and rivers and wetlands. Each biome has a certain type of climate and is characterized by its plant and animal life, which is adapted to live in the conditions it offers.

This book looks at life in the rain forest biome and the threats rain forests face today. It also looks at some solutions to these threats that may protect what is left of the natural world.

What Is a Rain Forest?

Rain forests, as their name suggests, are forests that grow in parts of the world that receive a lot of rainfall. This refers to places in which rainfall occurs consistently throughout the year, rather than regions that see heavy rain for just part of the year. The term usually refers to tropical rain forests, which are found near the equator. But there is also another type of rain forest—the temperate rain forest—found on North America's northwest coast, on the South Island of New Zealand, and in southern Chile.

Tropical Rain Forests

Tropical rain forests grow in Central and South America, Africa, Asia, and Australia in a belt that follows the equator across these continents. Although they grow in regions widely spread out across the globe, all tropical rain forests show very similar characteristics. They are all ancient and complex environments, needing a climate that provides constant daily rain—with a total of at least 59 inches (150 cm) a year—and a uniform temperature of about 82 °F (28 °C). There are no real seasons in rain forests. The weather feels the same—warm and humid—year-round. Rain forests all share another characteristic as well: all are under threat from human activity and are being cut down at an alarming rate around the world.

Constant Growth

All tropical rain forests show a great diversity of life. Between 50 and 200 different types of trees may be found on just 2.5 acres (1 ha) of rain forest. That is 20 times the species found in the most diverse temperate forest. Rain forest trees are mainly evergreen and have broad leaves, many with "drip tips" for shedding water. The trees lose old leaves but grow new ones at the same time, so they are never leafless. The forests are crowded, and trees grow to enormous heights—often 195 to 295 feet (60–90 m)—in their struggle to catch the light. Their roots are often very distinctive, having evolved to hold up the tall trees in soil that is often shallow and of poor quality. The results are huge buttress roots that prop the tree up from its base and amazing-looking stilt roots that stick out from the side of the tree into the ground. The forests also support huge climbing plants, including tough, woody vines called lianas, which can be 650 feet (200 m) long.

Persistent rain and abundant sunlight promote constant growth in tropical rain forests. Unlike forests farther from the equator, the growing season never stops here. Consider winter in America or Europe: leaves fall off most trees, daylight lessens, and the natural world goes into hibernation. Nothing like this happens in a tropical rain forest.

Green Forest

The lush green of the rain forest around Lake Sandoval in southern Peru, South America. Fed by the Madre de Dios River, this region sits within the Tambopata-Candamo reserve.

Dense Growth

Dense foliage in the Caribbean National Forest of Puerto Rico. This small region of tropical rain forest has been protected since the 1870s and is one of the earliest examples of a reserve.

An Amazing Habitat

Tropical rain forests produce half of the world's living wood. They are also home to about half of the world's species of plants and animals—and those are just the ones we know about, as scientists are still finding new species hidden away in the depths of these dense, green environments. Rain forests occupy about 7 percent of the land worldwide, yet they contain 80 percent of all the green vegetable matter that exists on land. All of the living, dead, and decaying trees and plants are called plant biomass. Scientists have figured out that a rain forest has around 49,600 tons (45,000 t) of plant biomass in every square mile (2.6 sq km), which is more than any other habitat on Earth. Each square yard (0.8 sq m) in a rain forest produces about four and a half pounds (2 kg) of new plant growth every year. Typical farmland, by comparison, produces around one and a half pounds (0.7 kg). This means that rain forests produce about 66 percent more green matter than farmland does.

Trees are the foundation of the rain forest. They provide food, shelter, and precious nutrients when they die and decompose. Take the trees away, and nothing else—not even the soil in which they grow—will survive.

Temperate Rain Forests

Temperate rain forests grow in wet, temperate climates in coastal regions around the world. The trees, plants, and animals found in temperate rain forests are very different from those found in tropical rain forests. Although they are smaller overall, temperate rain forests have suffered from human exploitation in much the same way as tropical rain forests.

Temperate rain forests are characterized by huge and often very ancient trees, such as the Douglas fir and Sitka spruce. Temperate rain forests in northwestern America have been called "Cathedral Forests" because of their enormous height—up to 280 feet (85 m)—and the great sense of space beneath their branches. Long gray-green epiphytes, plants that grow not from the ground but off of other plants, hang from trees in these forests, and because the climate is so damp, **mosses** grow on everything. Usually, there are many rotting branches and trees on the ground.

Temperate rain forests are full of long-established plant life called old growth. In Oregon and Washington, it is estimated that between 80 and 90 percent of the old growth has been cut down in the last few hundred years. This is a great loss, as it takes at least 200 years for this complex habitat to mature. Many creatures have suffered from the loss of temperate rain forests and some have been put on the endangered species list.

Threatened Species

The northern spotted owl, a threatened species that lives in the old growth temperate rain forests of America's Pacific Northwest. More than 80 percent of its habitat has been cut down.

9

A Green Environment

The tropical rain forest is a green world. The green leaves of the forest's plants and trees interact with the intense sunlight and the plentiful rain to provide the primary source of all energy in this environment. Therefore, the color green not only defines the rain forest environment; it is the very source of its existence.

The Different Layers

Tropical rain forests are typically structured in four layers. The lowest layer is the forest floor. The thick foliage above the floor shuts out most sunlight, so not many plants grow here, although fungi flourish in this environment, as do many types of ferns, which thrive in shade and moisture. Where large forest trees have fallen and allowed sunlight to penetrate to the forest floor, shrubs and smaller trees take advantage and spring up. The sparse vegetation of the forest floor makes it relatively easy for animals to move around, and this level is home to many of the larger animals of the rain forest, such as gorillas, jaguars, anteaters, wild boars, and tapirs. Snakes, such as the anaconda, which can grow up to 33 feet (10 m) long; spiders, such as the red-kneed tarantula and the large bird-eating spider; small mammals; and even some birds have all adapted to life on the forest floor. They need good eyesight and keen senses of smell and hearing to survive here.

The next layer up is called the under canopy. It is made up of small plants and trees, as well as the underside of the leaves of larger plants. It is mostly dark and damp, making it the least inhabited part of the forest. Plants such as ferns and vines growing from and supported by trees do well here, though.

Rain Forest Cat

The jaguar is the biggest cat found in South America, weighing up to 250 pounds (120 kg). It lives and hunts in the rain forests.

Human Evolution

Scientists have discovered that humans can distinguish between more shades of green than any other color. It is thought that the reason for this lies in our evolutionary past. As a species, we evolved over thousands of years in dense forests. It was essential for our survival to make out different greens underneath the canopy so that we could spot plants that were good to eat, see the movement of predators and game, and find trails.

Insects such as beetles and bees and some snakes and lizards hunt on the tree trunks and branches. Some birds make their nests here, and the occasional big cat, such as the jaguar, will lie in the branches keeping an eye out for prey on the floor below.

The next layer up, the canopy, is between 65 and 130 feet (20–40 m) high and is one of the most abundant parts of the forest. It consists of the foliage of trees and forms a roof for the forest. Many animals

live in the canopy—including monkeys, orangutans, sloths, frogs, and snakes—and never touch or go near the forest floor. The insects that live in the canopy are the least investigated and cataloged type of animal in the forest.

The highest level, called the emergent layer, is made up of the few very tall trees that have burst out of the canopy and stand on their own—260 feet (80 m) or more above the forest floor. These trees have fought their way to the top, and their reward is plenty of sunlight. Animals such as the green-winged macaw and the colobus monkey live high in the emergent trees and never see the lower regions. The harpy eagle, one of the largest eagles in the world, makes its nest high up in this layer but swoops down to feed on animals that live in the canopy.

Hunter at Risk

The harpy eagle is an endangered bird of prey and one of the largest types of eagles in the world, with a wingspan of more than six feet (2 m). Its habitat is the threatened rain forest of South America.

Carnivorous Plants

*Some plants living in the rain forest have insects on their menu. The soil they grow in is so thin and low in nutrients that they have to supplement their diet. The pitcher plant is one such carnivorous plant. It attracts its prey by its color and the scent of its sweet nectar, a liquid plant food that most insects find irresistible. However, the edge of the pitcher plant is steep and slippery. When an insect lands to feast on the nectar, it falls into a liquid inside the plant that contains **enzymes**. The enzymes digest the insect, and the plant absorbs it as food.*

Gliding Around

Animals living high up in the trees of the rain forest have developed different tactics for moving around. Monkeys have four limbs and a **prehensile** tail, which is so useful to them that it is like a fifth limb. Some animals can leap and glide through the air, landing on lower trees. The flying tree snake from Southeast Asia does not actually fly, but it too can glide through the air by using its muscles to make its body broader to catch more lift. Other animals that can glide include the flying lizard, which has a flap of skin under its front legs that it uses to glide, and the flying frog, which has flaps of skin on all four feet that catch the air as it leaps out of trees to avoid predators.

Unique Species

Rain forests all over the world are home to animals and plants that have evolved there and are found nowhere else on Earth. These are called endemic species. Often, they have evolved to fill a **niche** in the rain forest. The golden beetle, for example, exists only in the forests of Costa Rica, living on leaves and rotting plants. Islands are particularly rich in endemic species because they are cut off from the mainland. The island of Madagascar, off the coast of Africa, has more endemic species in its rain forests than any other place on Earth. Endemic animals and plants are especially at risk because they live in such a confined region. Once wiped out in a certain area, their gene pool is gone from Earth forever.

Rare Lemurs

Ring-tailed lemurs live in the forests of Madagascar. They are on the endangered species list due to habitat destruction by people living on the island.

Where Rain Forests Are Found

In spite of their huge importance to all life on this planet, tropical rain forests grow only in a narrow band all around the world. This stretches north from the equator as far as the tropic of Cancer and south as far as the tropic of Capricorn. This is because the climatic conditions—constant warmth from the sun and a year-round supply of precipitation—exist only between the tropics. However, rain forests are found on four of the seven continents on Earth: Central and South America, Africa, Asia, and Australia.

Central and South America

More than half of the world's tropical rain forests are found in Central and South America in countries such as Mexico, Brazil, Belize, Guatemala, Costa Rica, Colombia, and Ecuador. The mightiest rain forest of all, Brazil's Amazon rain forest, is found here. It covers an estimated 1,930,550 square miles (5 million sq km) and is home to 30 percent of all known plant and animal species. There are many mammals, such as the jaguar, sloth, tapir, and many types of monkeys, including the most agile of all, the spider monkey, and the loudest of all, the howler monkey. Birds are everywhere, creating an enormous variety of color and noise. Among them are harpy eagles, macaws, toucans, honeycreepers, and sun conures. Hunting among the foliage and in the rivers are reptiles such as lizards, caimans, and snakes,

including the 20-foot (6 m) boa constrictor and the poisonous coral snake. Amphibians, such as the brightly colored poison arrow frog, are also found here.

Central and South American rain forests are shrinking due to continued exploitation by humans. Some 25,000 square miles (65,000 sq km) of rain forest are disappearing from this region every year. Logging and clearing trees for farmland on which to grow such crops as rice, sugarcane, soybeans, and bananas are two of the main causes.

Southeast Asia

Southeast Asia features a rich and varied region of tropical rain forests in countries equally diverse—Cambodia, the Philippines, China, Indonesia, Myanmar, and Malaysia. Animals found in these rain forests include mammals such as tapirs, tarsiers (a type of lemur), orangutans, gibbons, colobine monkeys, tigers, tree shrews, flying foxes, and bamboo rats. There are birds such as hawk eagles, tree swifts, fairy bluebirds, fantails, whistlers,

Huge Reptile

The black caiman, the largest member of the alligator family, lives in rivers and wetlands of the rain forests of central South America. It can grow to more than 13 feet (4 m) in length.

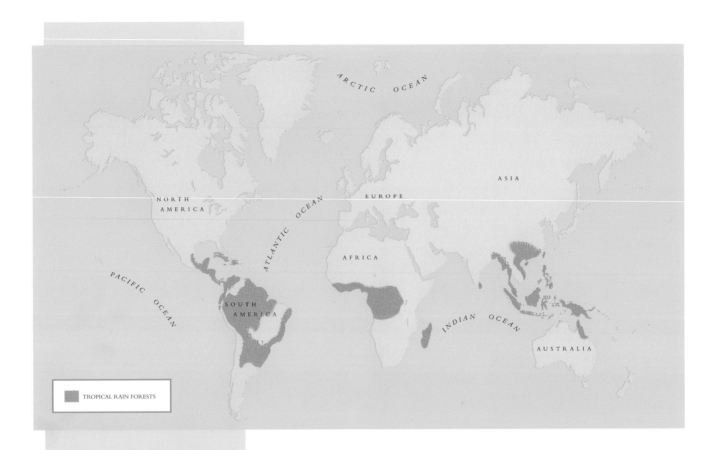

TROPICAL RAIN FORESTS

World Rain Forests

A map showing the main rain forest regions of the world.

flowerpeckers, and wood swallows; insects such as Malayan frog beetles, Queen Alexandra's birdwing butterflies, and Goliath birdwing butterflies; and reptiles such as green cat snakes and water dragons.

Like the forests of Central and South America, these rain forests have been reduced in size, mainly because of logging, farming, and mining. With so much habitat under threat, many animals have suffered. The orangutan, for example, once lived throughout the rain forests of China and Malaysia but is now found only on the islands of Sumatra and Borneo.

The island of New Guinea is about 70 to 90 percent rain forest and includes tropical swamps and **mangroves**. Yet even here the forest is in danger. As the human population has grown, so have the effects of small-scale agriculture. And with logging and mining companies moving in and commercial plantation crops increasing, even this large island paradise is threatened by 21st-century progress.

Africa

Rain forests are found in the Congo basin in central Africa and on the coast of western Africa in the countries of Ghana, the Ivory Coast, and Senegal. Animals of African rain forests include mammals such as antelopes, chimpanzees, gorillas, scaly-tailed squirrels, duikers, okapi (a mammal related to, but smaller than, the giraffe), hippopotamuses, black-and-white colobus monkeys, bush babies, pygmy hippos, and bats. Birds such as Senegal parrots, Congo peafowl, African gray parrots, and scarlet-chested sunbirds also live here.

Africa's coastal forests have been extensively reduced and today exist only in small pockets that are very accessible to loggers and farmers. Rain forests in the Congo basin have faired better, partly because of their greater isolation.

Threatened Gorillas

A huge male mountain gorilla. These endangered animals live in the high forests of Rwanda, Zaire, and Uganda in central Africa. There are thought to be fewer than 400 left in the wild.

Australian Platypus

A close-up of the duck-billed platypus. This primitive mammal burrows in riverbanks in the forests of eastern Australia.

Australia

Australian rain forests are found on the coastal fringes in the far north and northeast of the country in Queensland and the Northern Territories. They are home to some of the most unique animals on Earth, found nowhere else. These include mammals such as tree kangaroos, rat kangaroos, opossums, bandicoots, and duck-billed platypuses. Birds include cassowaries, brolgas, orange-footed scrubfowls, wompoo fruit doves, topknot pigeons, Australian king parrots, laughing kookaburras, and fernwrens. Reptile life includes frilled lizards, carpet pythons, green tree snakes, spotted tree monitors, eastern water dragons, and northern leaf-tailed geckos. Insects native to Australia include Ulysses butterflies, zodiac moths, Union Jack butterflies, and birdwing butterflies. Amphibians are represented by White's tree frogs, giant tree frogs, striped marsh frogs, northern barred frogs, and dainty green tree frogs.

The rain forests of Queensland have been fragmented by logging and road-building companies and by farmers looking for more land for their dairy cattle and crops. Some of the forest is now under government protection.

Temperate Rain Forests

Temperate rain forests need a unique set of environmental circumstances to flourish. These include a high rainfall of 6.6 feet (2 m) or more every year, mild winters, and cool summers around 59 °F (15 °C). These conditions exist in only a few places on Earth:

• The northwest coast of North America (Oregon, Washington, and Alaska in the United States and British Colombia in Canada)
• The southwestern coast of Tasmania, Australia
• Fiordland National Park on South Island, New Zealand
• The southwest coast of Chile
• The coast of Japan
• The southwest coast of Norway
• The Black Sea coast of Turkey and Georgia

The special climate allows the trees in these forests to grow to an immense size. Unfortunately, this has made their wood highly prized by loggers, who have felled the forests in many areas for years.

Moss and Ferns

Large ferns and trees covered in moss are typical vegetation found in temperate rain forests. This photograph shows the protected Hoh River valley in Olympic National Park in Washington.

Why Tropical Rain Forests Are Important

Some people wonder why so much fuss is made in the news about the plight of the rain forests. After all, Earth is a huge and dynamic planet in a state of constant change. In its billions of years of history, it has gone from a barren rock to home to millions of types of life-forms. However, take a look at the 10 rain forest facts below and consider the implications of the rain forests' disappearance.

1 Rain forests are a major source of timber and are therefore of commercial value.
2 They are a source of medicine and drugs, taken from the bark, roots, and leaves of trees and plants.
3 They are a source of food, oils, spices, gums, dyes, and natural rubber.
4 The roots of their trees help bind the precious and fragile soils of the landscape.
5 Rain forests regulate and help purify the world's water.
6 They enable three-quarters of the world's water to reenter the atmosphere through **evaporation** and **transpiration** in a vast and complex process known as the **water cycle**.
7 They are a major influence on the world's climate.
8 They play a major role in the **oxygen cycle**.
9 They are the most diverse and rich habitat in the world.
10 They are a main part of the world's life-support system.

Rain Forest Crop

This farmer is harvesting sugarcane near his village in the northern Philippines. Sugarcane is a rain forest plant.

Economic Value

Some rain forest trees are extremely valuable to the modern world. Rubber trees provide people with latex, the milky juice found underneath their bark, to make rubber. Hardwoods such as teak and mahogany are highly prized for furniture.

Rain forests are also a great source of food. People have survived in the forests for thousands of years, living off their natural produce. Many rain forest food products are today used all over the world. Some of the most common products include chocolate (from the cocoa plant), sugarcane, sweet potatoes, pineapples, oranges, lemons, bananas, mangos, Brazil nuts, cashews, peanuts, yams, papayas, guavas, avocadoes, coffee, and spices such as nutmeg, ginger, and cloves.

In addition to providing food and other products, jungle plants have given people some very powerful chemicals and drugs. The rain forest has been called the largest drug store in the world.

Cocoa Harvest

This man is harvesting cocoa pods, the raw ingredient of chocolate. The cocoa plant originally came from the rain forests of South America, but today it is grown in Africa, Sri Lanka, and Southeast Asia.

Almost a quarter of all the medicines in the developed world have come from them. Often, the clues about these medicines' benefits were given to scientists by native people who, through trial and error, discovered many healing uses for various plants. The common painkiller aspirin originally came from the bark of a rain forest tree, and quinine—a drug used to help cure **malaria**— came from the red cinchona tree found in South America. The rosy periwinkle, from the island of Madagascar, contains chemicals that have helped fight two forms of cancer in humans: Hodgkin's disease and leukemia. Today, one of the most persuasive arguments for halting the destruction of the rain forests is that such destruction may be causing the extinction of useful plants that scientists know nothing about. In the process, people may be losing life-saving medicines provided by nature for free.

Influence on Climate and Water

Rain forests have an effect on both the local and the international climate and water supply. On a regional scale, as rain forest trees put water back into the atmosphere, they help create clouds, which, in turn, produce more rain in the region, helping to maintain the rain forest climate. As rain forest trees absorb water through their roots and release it back into the atmosphere, they also filter out impurities in the water.

On a worldwide scale, rain forest trees not only help maintain a healthy balance in the water cycle, but they also take carbon dioxide out of the atmosphere through the process of photosynthesis. **Carbon** gets stored in the living tissue of the trees, and oxygen is put back into the atmosphere. This process is essential to the health of the planet, since carbon dioxide is the main **greenhouse gas** contributing to the gradual warming up of the world's climate.

The Richest Habitat

One of the reasons tropical rain forests are so precious is that they harbor more varieties of plant and animal life than just about any other type of habitat on Earth. In fact, the Amazon rain forest is the most species-rich environment on the planet. It contains 80,000 species of trees and 2,000 species of freshwater fish,

Photosynthesis

*Photosynthesis is the process by which green plants turn water and sunlight into carbohydrates and oxygen. Only green plants can carry out photosynthesis, because the **chlorophyll** that makes their leaves look green is a chemical vital to the process. Through photosynthesis, rain forest plants produce 40 percent of Earth's oxygen.*

Food from Leaves

A highly magnified photograph of a chloroplast, part of the structure of a leaf that contains chlorophyll. Chloroplasts are vital to food production through photosynthesis in green plants.

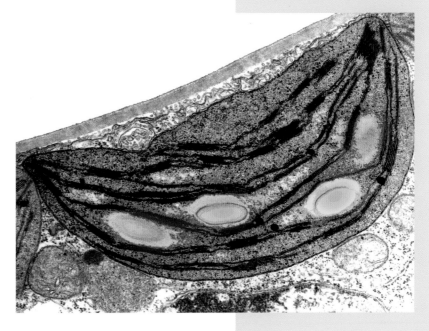

Rain Forest Fish

A photograph of a piranha, clearly showing the razor-sharp teeth it is famous for. These fish are native to the freshwater rivers and lakes of tropical central South America.

including the infamous piranha. The area is also home to half of the world's known species of butterflies—about 9,000—including monarch, malachite, and postman butterflies, and more than 3,000 land vertebrate species.

In Queensland, in northeast Australia, the small belt of rain forest that covers only one-tenth of a percent of the total land area contains a high percentage of the overall number of species in the country. It is home to 37 different **marsupial** species, including the tree kangaroo, musky rat kangaroo, and spotted-tailed quoll (a small, meat-eating marsupial); 47 different types of frogs; and 62 percent of the country's butterflies, including several huge species, such as the *Aenetus monabilis*, with its 7-inch (18 cm) wingspan, and the Hercules moth, with an even bigger 10-inch (25 cm) wingspan. This part of Australia also has the greatest diversity of bird life in the country, featuring 370 known species with such exotic names as the tooth-billed catbird and bridled honeyeater.

Similarly, the rain forests of Costa Rica in Central America are among the most diverse habitats on Earth. Although more than half of the overall forest area has been cut down since Europeans arrived in the country in the 16th century, there is still enough rain forest left to harbor around 215 types of mammals, 560 species of birds, 250 kinds of reptiles, and 115 species of fish. Some of these species are on the world's endangered list. Costa Rica features 11 bird species on this list, including the harpy eagle, crested eagle, and orange-breasted falcon.

Counting Species

Counting species is not easy and has long been a subject of hot debate among scientists. More than one and a half million species have been recorded worldwide. However, scientists know that there are many more that are yet undiscovered. It has been estimated that there are between 2 million and 80 million total species of plants and animals on Earth today, with most scientists leaning toward the 10 million mark.

Most of the identified species are mammals and birds. This is because they tend to be quite large and relatively easily seen and classified. Most of the animals and plants remaining to be classified are small: insects, worms, and fungi. Searching for new species in the depths of a rain forest is difficult, but this is where many of them are to be found.

Tiny Amphibian

A strawberry poison dart frog inside a mushroom in Costa Rica. These tiny animals live in the rain forests of Central America.

Zaire is a country in south-central Africa that has avoided some of the spectacular destruction of the rain forest that many other areas have experienced. About three-quarters of the original tree cover of the landscape in Zaire remains intact today, and the country is like one huge nature reserve, with more types of birds and mammals than any other country in Africa. However, a road-building program has given people better access to more remote areas, leading to an increase in logging activity in the country.

Rain Forests Under Threat

Rain forests all over the world are under attack. The reasons are simple. Rain forests do not produce much wealth for local people or governments. Felling timber, especially for wood from valuable hardwoods such as mahogany, makes some money. But, by far, the most profitable thing to do with the land is to clear it for farming. Profits can also be made by mining, extracting oil, and even hunting animals to sell as pets or to use their fur.

Our Shrinking Forests

Rain forests have been shrinking for 100 years or more. They once covered about 14 percent of Earth's surface. In the worst decade for rain forest destruction, from 1980 to 1990, almost 65,640 square miles (170,000 sq km) of rain forest were destroyed every year. To put this in perspective, an area the size of New England was lost annually. By 1991, half of the world's tropical rain forests had been destroyed. And in the last decade, about 15 percent more has been lost for good. At this rate of destruction, there will be no tropical rain forests left by the middle of the 21st century.

Sacred Bird

The resplendent quetzal, a bird once sacred to the Mayan civilization of Central America and now the national bird of Guatemala. It is on the endangered species list due to rain forest felling and hunting.

Clearing Land

Slash and burn agriculture has been practiced for hundreds of years in the rain forests by tribal societies. Today, it is used more aggressively by modern farmers to clear land of trees to grow crops.

Slash and Burn

The life of the great rain forests forms a complex web, both fragile and remarkably resilient. It can cope with certain amounts of change and even damage. For example, humans have lived in these forests for many thousands of years, practicing slash and burn agriculture. They make small clearings in the forest by cutting and burning the foliage, and then they settle and grow their crops. Usually, after a few years, they move on to another part of the forest. This allows the forest to recover and regrow. Using this method of agriculture, the level of human interference in the life of the forest remained small and containable for many years.

Today, however, industrial-scale logging and road building into the heart of once-remote areas means that change is happening at a speed and level that the natural environment cannot handle. Even slash and burn agriculture has added to **deforestation** due to the rise in human population. With more people doing it, even this primitive practice has become a problem for the forest.

Soil Loss

Tropical rain forests are supported mostly by thin soils only an inch (2.5 cm) or so deep in places. If there is plenty of tree cover, this is not a problem, since tree roots and other plants help keep the soil in place. This soil is replenished by the natural cycle of death and decay; branches, leaves, insects, animals, and birds all eventually die and fall to the forest floor, where termites and fungi help them to decompose. Because of the jungle's heat and humidity, decomposition and the release of precious nutrients back into the growing cycle occur relatively quickly.

However, when trees are cut down, powerful tropical rains soon sweep away the vulnerable soil, causing infertility. Even if trees are replanted, it takes 50 years or more for the soil to recover. Cutting down large areas of rain forest can also increase the number of floods that occur in the region. This is because trees help hold on to water, both in their roots and within their leaves. Without them, rainwater can pour across the landscape.

The Changing Rain Forest

A changed landscape in Peru —ancient, virgin rain forest and land cleared for farming adjoin each other. A new road provides loggers and farmers with access to even more remote parts of the rain forest.

Lost to Farming

A section of the Amazon rain forest being felled and burned to provide space for cattle farmers.

Non-sustainable Farming

People have cleared huge areas of rain forest to graze cattle. However, this has proved **unsustainable**; within a decade, the land is useless. It has lost all of its nutrients, and farmers have to move elsewhere to graze their cattle, felling more trees to do so, and leaving behind a small desert in the process. Such **desertification** occurs for several reasons. The most important is that the trees have been removed, so the soil is easily washed away. In addition, cattle eat the groundcover and prevent any regrowth, and their hooves damage the thin soils.

Logging in Indonesia

Indonesia, a country in tropical Southeast Asia, is made up of more than 13,000 islands and has a population of more than 200 million people. There are about 300 different ethnic groups, including many tribal peoples from the extensive rain forests that carpet vast areas of these islands. Today, loggers bulldoze dirt roads that penetrate into the heart of remote and previously inaccessible forests, home to native tribes that have lived in isolation for hundreds, if not thousands, of years.

Once roads have cut lines of communication into the dense forests, local hunters and farmers move in to exploit the opportunity they provide. They build small homes that then become more permanent. Eventually, small settlements grow in the forests and turn into larger villages, and the remoteness of the area is lost forever. New areas are cleared for further farming, native peoples are driven away, and wildlife comes under increased threat. Erosion follows the clearing of the trees, and, eventually, the land becomes barren. This process is not unique to Indonesia. It is fairly typical of all tropical rain forest regions.

Destruction of the Amazon Rain Forest

The Amazon rain forest is not only the largest rain forest in the world; it is also one of the most ravaged. As with many other forests, road-building deep into the heart of the landscape has opened the door to further development by farmers, miners, and loggers. Much of the most destructive development started in the 1960s and was financed by the **World Bank**. The Trans-Amazonian highway (Belem-Brasilia highway) was built more than 40 years ago and proved to be the first of the huge roads that opened up the heart of the rain forest. It was part of a government program to move poor, landless people from the more populated south and east portions of Brazil onto land cleared in the rain forests. Deforestation increased a great deal during the 1970s and 1980s as room was made for these new settlers. Native peoples in very small numbers had lived in Rondonia, a region in the far west of the country, for thousands of years. Suddenly, from the 1970s onward, more than 50,000 people a year were arriving to open up the land and farm. This massive change put enormous pressure on the land resources, especially the thin rain forest soils.

Growing Soybeans

In a world in which farmers produce food for markets thousands of miles away, land use can change very quickly to suit the tastes of consumers. Today, many people in Europe feel that eating soybean products is good for their health. The beans are low in fat and cholesterol and make a good substitute for milk and cheese. Many soybean crops grown in the U.S. have been genetically modified, which is not what European consumers want. As a result, farmers living in rain forest regions in South America have started growing non-genetically modified soybeans for European markets. Although they can make a good profit with these crops, they must clear a lot of rain forest land to grow them. In Paraguay alone, almost 2.5 million acres (1 million ha) of rain forest have been cleared in the last 10 years.

Lemur at Risk

Verreaux's sifaka lemur, found in the wild only on the island of Madagascar, is currently on the vulnerable species list.

Endangered Animals of the Rain Forest

The number of endangered species in the rain forests is increasing. This is due to the destruction of their homes and overhunting. Here is a short list of just some of these animals. And don't forget that plants are endangered as well.

- *Aye aye, a small **primate** from the island of Madagascar*
- *Boa constrictor, from Central and South America*
- *Caiman, a reptile from Central and South America*
- *Congo peacock, from Africa*
- *Golden lion tamarin, a mammal from the forests of Brazil*
- *Gorilla, from the African countries of Zaire, Rwanda, and Uganda*
- *Harpy eagle, from Central and South America*
- *Jaguar, from Central and South America*
- *Kinkajou, a small, **nocturnal** mammal from Central and South America*
- *Lemur, a small primate from Madagascar*
- *Loris, a primate from Southeast Asia*
- *Okapi, a mammal from the forests of central Africa*
- *Orangutan, from the Southeast Asian islands of Borneo and Sumatra*
- *Queen Alexandra's birdwing butterfly, found only in certain forests in Papua New Guinea*
- *Scarlet macaw, from Central and South America*
- *Tapir, a mammal from Asia and Central and South America*
- *Tarsier, a small mammal from the Philippines and Indonesia*

Endangered Species

The World Conservation Union is an organization formed in 1948 by the United Nations. Its original name was the International Union for the Conservation of Nature and Natural Resources, or IUCN. This organization produces and updates a list of plants and animals around the world that it classifies as endangered. It keeps this information in what is called *The Red Book*. This book lists more than 12,000 individual endangered species, many of which are found in rain forests around the world, and most of which are plants. The endangered species count rose by 2,000 species from 2002 to 2003. This rapid increase may be explained in part by scientists being better able to study and record species than they were in the past. However, there can be no doubt that the movement toward extinction is speeding up in part because change brought about by human activity is accelerating all over the world.

Hunted to the Brink

The tapir is a secretive mammal related to the rhinoceros. It lives in the jungles of Central and South America and Southeast Asia. It has a small trunk, thick and hairy skin, and a short tail. Tapirs grow up to three feet (0.9 m) tall and live off plants. They do not breed often, so their population remains small. Due to the destruction of their forest home, and because people hunt them for their meat, they are becoming endangered. The Baird's tapir, for example, is now extinct in El Salvador and Mexico, where it once lived near the river edges of the dense forests.

Tapir Threatened

A photograph of the elusive and endangered Baird's tapir, taken in Corcovado National Park in Costa Rica. This mammal likes to live in the heart of the rain forest, close to water.

Trees in Danger

Plants, including trees, make up the biggest group on the list of endangered species. They are the habitat that provides a home for animals. So when we talk about animals suffering from habitat destruction, it means that trees and plants are being chopped down. One example of this is the caoba tree, found in the Ecuadorian lowland forests. It is a relative of the avocado tree and has been felled for its timber. However, it recently has been cut down in large quantities to make way for banana trees and oil palms—crops that are worth far more money than the caoba tree. This conversion of native forest into plantation crops is an increasingly common problem in rain forests worldwide.

Hunted Almost to Extinction

The skins of illegally hunted big cats are confiscated by customs officers. Tigers once ranged through central and southern Asian rain forests and grasslands but have been hunted to near-extinction.

The Future for Rain Forests

Aside from the many scientific reasons to hold on to rain forests, such as their role in regulating the world's climate, purifying and recycling our water, and providing a home for millions of animals, there are also moral questions to be faced concerning the destruction of this habitat. For example, do we have the right to destroy such a fragile but fertile environment? Future generations surely have the right to inherit these wonderful places. "This we know: the Earth does not belong to man; man belongs to the Earth. All things are connected like the blood that unites us all. Man did not weave the web of life; he is merely a strand in it. Whatever he does to the web, he does to himself." These are the words of Chief Seattle, a Native American, and they remind us that we have an obligation not to degrade Earth beyond repair, but to take only what we need, so that areas such as rain forests can replenish themselves.

At the same time, people who live in or near rain forests have the right to earn a living. These forests grow mostly in relatively poor countries, where every dollar counts. Because the governments of these nations are not rich, they cannot always afford to protect rain forests from exploitation from farming, logging, and hunting, since some of the money

Threatened Peoples

A pygmy girl from the rain forests of Zaire (previous page). Her people have lived throughout equatorial countries in Africa for thousands of years.

Balanced Lives

Yanomami tribespeople preparing the staple root food, manioc, out of which they make a type of bread. The Yanomami have lived in the rain forests of Brazil and Venezuela for thousands of years without disrupting the ecology of their environment.

Rich and Poor

*Most tropical rain forests are found in Third World, or developing, countries. These are poor countries in which the people are mainly farmers struggling to survive in a **global economy**. Clearing rain forests to make cropland is one way for people to increase their income. It is unfair to expect such people to see the problems in the same way people from rich countries see them. As one farmer said, "If the West [Europe and the U.S.] wants us to grow trees, then they will have to pay us to do so."*

earned from these activities is paid directly to the government as a form of tax. Some of these taxes are used to pay for necessities such as clean water, hospitals, schools, and public transportation. Protecting the remaining rain forests while also allowing local people to live their lives and farm their land is one of the biggest concerns facing the world in the 21st century.

Too Little But Not Too Late

It has been estimated that only 10 percent of the world's rain forests are currently under any form of protection. Scientists believe this is too little to save forests as a habitat with all of their important **biodiversity**. However, they also believe that there is still time for the people of the world to come together to do something about it and increase the amount of forest protected.

World Bank Initiative

The World Bank was set up in 1945, after World War II. It is run by the United Nations, and it has lent money to poorer countries to help them develop industry and farming. This has caused problems for rain forests in places such as Brazil, where World Bank money was used to build roads deep into the jungle. However, the World Bank recently joined forces with the World Wide Fund for Nature (WWF) to create a program called Forest Alliance. This partnership aims to increase the number of rain forests worldwide that are protected from exploitation. Working with governments and private industry to make sure that the forests are properly managed will help to stop the extinction of plants and animals in rain forests. The Forest Alliance plans to create 124 million acres (50 million ha) of new protected forest and to implement effective ways to monitor the areas.

Saving Birds

More birds are threatened with extinction in the rain forests of Central and South America and in Southeast Asia than in any other part of the world. The latest figures show that there are 113 different species in Brazil and 115 species in Indonesia that are threatened. Today, there are dozens of conservation areas throughout Indonesia and Brazil. For example, Mount Leuser National Park on the island of Sumatra covers 3,670 square miles (9,500 sq km) and is one of the largest conservation areas in all of Southeast Asia.

Help for the Orangutan

Baby orangutans have been prized by local forest hunters and **poachers** in Indonesia for many years. This is because people will pay a lot of money to have one as a pet. Before taking the baby away, the hunters first kill the mother, who will otherwise fiercely protect her offspring. This has led to a dramatic decline in the population of orangutans in the wild. Because of this, the government of Indonesia has now banned people from owning pet orangutans.

To help those animals that have spent time in captivity, rehabilitation centers have been set up. The goal is to educate these primates in the ways of the wild so that they can go back into the jungle on their own. First, the orangutan is taken to the edge of the forest and allowed to do some exploring, while still fed by its keepers. Then the keepers withhold food for a few days, and the animal has to try to gather its own food from the forest, like its wild relatives would do. The program has been moderately successful. Many tame orangutans will never really be able to fend for themselves in the jungle. The best that can be achieved is a semi-wild state in which they are fed and live in protected areas.

Protected Species

This mother and baby orangutan have been saved from the hunters that have devastated the orangutan population in Indonesia. They have been released into the Tanjung Puting Biosphere Reserve in Borneo.

Australia Leads the Way

In 1988, a vast area of rain forest in Queensland was made a **World Heritage Site**. It covers almost 3,475 square miles (9,000 sq km) and includes 43 different forest areas and 41 national parks. The project was opposed at first by the Queensland government because it gave a high level of protection to the forest, which was in conflict with the interests of loggers and farmers. However, tourism is becoming an increasing form of income for the area, helped by the proximity of the rain forests to beautiful sandy beaches, a wide ocean, and the **Great Barrier Reef**, which is also a World Heritage Site. The region also contains the only surviving native Aboriginal Australian rain forest people. They now inhabit a protected reserve called the Yarrabah Aboriginal Reserve.

It has been estimated that 20 percent of the original forest cover in the region is now gone, but that still leaves a substantial area of this precious habitat. It is still logged and farmed, but these activities are monitored and carried out in a sustainable manner. In many ways, this is an excellent example for the future. However, Australia is a relatively rich country. The protection rain forests get in this country is likely to be hard to duplicate in poorer, developing countries.

Forest Parks

A woman walking in the rain forest in Daintree National Park in Queensland, Australia. The park was created in 1988 to protect this ancient forest region.

Costa Rica's Amistad Biosphere Reserve

Costa Rican forests have suffered ever since the arrival of Spanish explorers and settlers in the 16th century. More than half of the forests are now gone, along with many of the native Guaymi Indians who lived in them. Those forests remaining are under threat from copper mining, logging, beef farming, drilling, and poaching, as the government of Costa Rica, like so many governments in poor, developing countries, has encouraged farming and mining in forest areas.

Fortunately, centered on the mountainous region of the Cordillera de Talamanca in the heart of Costa Rica lies a special protected region called the Amistad **Biosphere Reserve**. Due to the protection offered by this reserve, the destruction has slowed down, and even the native peoples have increased in number, from around 6,000 in 1960 to more than 10,000 today. These are small but significant gains.

Cuban Reserve

A small frog sitting on a leaf in the Cuchillas del Toa Biosphere Reserve in Cuba. This special place was made a biosphere reserve in 1986.

Tourism in Madagascar

The island of Madagascar, off the southeast coast of Africa, has more endangered primates living in its rain forests than anywhere else on Earth. The island has had about 90 percent of its forest and plant cover cut down, so the original habitat of these primates has shrunk to a very small proportion. Today, Madagascar, which has more endemic animal species than any other country, is a popular **eco-tourism** destination. Thus, it is in the best interest of the Madagascan government to help save what remains of the rain forests and their biodiversity in order to keep tourists coming to their island.

Eco-tourism, a Model for the Future

Tourists spend billions of dollars every year on flights, car rentals, accommodations, restaurants, entertainment, and leisure sports while on vacation. Today, the tourism industry caters to all sorts of different people—from those who want culture and famous cities, to those who want to go deep-sea diving or rock climbing. One of the fastest-growing areas is eco-tourism. People who care about the environment and who want to spend time on vacation among wild animals and plants can choose to travel with companies that aim to minimize the impact they have on the places they visit. Vacationers can even opt for a working vacation during which they actively try to improve the landscape by planting trees, cleaning up litter, or taking part in monitoring birds, sea creatures, and plants.

Places as far apart as Cameroon and Costa Rica have become involved in eco-tourism. They have set up nature reserves, protecting their unique and beautiful wildlife and landscapes. These assets attract tourists, who pay to visit them. The income from tourism pays the wages of the wardens and other workers, helps maintain the nature reserves, and generates tax for the national government. It is hoped that this model will be used by many developing nations that have precious rain forests to preserve. Eco-tourism can become a serious contender to replace logging, destructive farming, and rare animal and plant poaching as a much-needed source of income for local communities.

Conservation Organizations

The first step in saving the rain forests is watching what we have now and monitoring it in the future. Today, there are many different organizations around the world dedicated to helping and monitoring the rain forest environment. Some are large and involve the help and funding of many countries; others are small and very local. Here are some of the more well-known organizations:

• **Friends of the Earth**   www.foe.org
Founded in 1971 in Britain, Friends of the Earth is now one of the world's best-known and most respected environmental pressure groups.
• **World Wide Fund for Nature (WWF)**   www.panda.org
Founded in 1961, this Swiss-based organization raises money to fund conservation operations around the world, focusing in particular on endangered animals.
• **Greenpeace**   www.greenpeace.org/usa/
Founded in 1971 in Canada, Greenpeace has grown to become one of the world's biggest and most influential environmental pressure groups. It campaigns all over the world on behalf of the environment.
• **International Union for the Conservation of Nature (IUCN)**   www.iucn.org
This organization publishes *The Red Book*, which presents the most comprehensive picture we have today of the state of the planet in terms of threats to species.

What You Can Do to Help

Everyone can get involved in helping to save rain forests. Many schools have projects supporting this special habitat. The first step is to become more informed about the situation. Here are a few ways you might help the rain forest biome:

• Be careful in selecting plants for your garden or as presents for friends and family. Some rain forest plants are very rare, and taking them from their natural setting to make a profit harms the forest. In some countries, it is illegal to sell rare plants.
• Get involved in efforts to raise people's awareness of the fragility of rain forest environments through projects at school or with local clubs.
• Get involved at school to find out more about the fascinating lives of rain forest animals and the wonderful plants that have evolved to survive in this warm and wet environment.
• Support one of the many environmental organizations dedicated to protecting rain forests. Fund-raising events and awareness days often feature fun activities.

• Have respect for the people who live in rain forest regions.

• Remember, whatever delicate natural environment you find yourself in, take nothing but photographs and leave nothing but footprints. That way, you will always leave wild places in the same state in which you found them.

Further Reading

Green, Jen. *Rain Forests*. Milwaukee, Wis.: Gareth Stevens, 1999.

Lasky, Kathryn. *The Most Beautiful Roof in the World: Exploring the Rainforest Canopy*. San Diego: Harcourt Brace & Co., 1997.

National Wilderness Federation. *Rain Forests*. New York: Learning Triangle Press, 1997.

Parker, Edward. *Rain Forest People*. Austin, Tex.: Raintree Steck-Vaughn, 2003.

Pyers, Greg. *Rain Forest Explorer*. Chicago: Raintree, 2005.

Welsbacher, Anne. *Life in a Rainforest*. Minneapolis: Lerner Publications, 2003.

Web sites

Rainforest Action Network
http://www.ran.org

The Rainforest Site
http://www.therainforestsite.org

Rainforests.net
http://www.rainforests.net

Tropical Rainforest Coalition
http://www.rainforest.org

Tropical Rainforests
http://rainforests.mongabay.com

What's It Like Where You Live?
http://mbgnet.mobot.org/sets/rforest/index.htm

Glossary

Biodiversity   The numbers and types of different plants and animals living in a specific environment.

Biosphere reserve   An internationally recognized conservation area administered by the United Nations Education, Scientific, and Cultural Organization (UNESCO).

Carbon   An element found in several forms and in combination with other elements to form compounds; combined with oxygen, it forms carbon dioxide. All living things have carbon in them.

Chlorophyll   A substance found in most plants that makes them green in color. It absorbs the energy from sunlight and makes it available to the plant for the production of carbohydrates.

Deforestation   The removal of forests and woodlands, usually by people. Reasons include clearing land for agriculture or industry and timber harvesting.

Desertification   Human actions that turn fertile land into sterile desert, through overgrazing, loss of vegetation, and soil erosion.

Eco-tourism   Tourism based upon a more sensitive approach to the impact that travelers have upon the landscapes they visit.

Enzymes   Substances found in the bodies of animals and plants that help certain life processes happen. For example, there are enzymes in the digestive system that help break down food.

Evaporation   When water is heated and turns into vapor, it is said to have evaporated. Evaporation is part of the water cycle.

Evolved   Scientists believe that life on Earth has developed, or evolved, over billions of years. The theory of evolution claims that all life has come from single-celled forms and has slowly become more complex.

Global economy   A term used to describe the fact that the economies of individual countries are linked to each other due to the high level of international trade that takes place in the modern world.

Great Barrier Reef   The largest group of coral reefs in the world. The Great Barrier Reef stretches for more than 1,240 miles (2,000 km) off the east coast of Australia.

Greenhouse gas   A gas, such as carbon dioxide or methane, that traps heat in Earth's atmosphere.

Habitats   Parts of an environment that are self-contained, supplying the needs of the organisms that live within them.

Malaria   A disease that is passed to humans through mosquito bites. It causes a very high recurring fever.

Mangroves   Muddy coastal wetlands in which mangrove trees grow.

Marsupial   A type of mammal, defined by a special pouch in which it carries its young. Examples are the kangaroo and the wallaby.

Mosses   Plants that do not have any flowers. There are more than 10,000 different species around the world.

Niche   The place within a habitat that each living organism occupies. This includes the way in which an animal or plant uses its habitat—what it eats, where it sleeps, and the environmental conditions it favors.

Nocturnal   Something that happens or is active at night. Some animals are described as being nocturnal, which means that they come out at night to hunt for food.

Oxygen cycle   The process by which animals breathe in oxygen and exhale carbon dioxide, and then plants convert the carbon dioxide back into oxygen, which they release into the atmosphere.

Poachers   People who illegally shoot animals for meat or to sell to other people as trophies.

Prehensile   Capable of gripping branches.

Primate   The highest order of mammals in the animal kingdom. Primates include monkeys, chimpanzees, and lemurs.

Temperate   A term used to describe a climate that is neither too hot nor too cold. Temperate zones are found halfway between the hot tropics and the cold poles.

Transpiration   The process by which water is lost through the leaves of plants and trees due to evaporation.

Tundra   Land close to or inside the Arctic Circle, where the layer of soil just below the surface is permanently frozen due to year-round low temperatures.

Unsustainable   Something that cannot be carried out indefinitely into the future.

Water cycle   The natural cycle in which water evaporates from bodies of water and is given out from plants into the atmosphere. Here it eventually condenses again to form clouds and precipitation.

World Bank   A special bank set up in 1945 after World War II to help restore the economies of the devastated countries. It is part of the United Nations.

World Heritage Site   A cultural or natural site that is considered to be of outstanding value to humanity. The World Heritage program is administered by UNESCO.

Index